The Book of Gingerbread

The Book of Gingerbread

Carla Capalbo

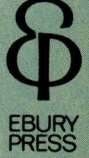

EBURY PRESS

Published by Ebury Press
National Magazine House
72 Broadwick Street
London W1V 2BP

First impression 1984

Edited, designed and illustrated by
the E T Archive Ltd, Chelsea Wharf,
15 Lots Road, London SW10 0QH

Designer Julian Holland
Photography Eileen Tweedy

PO Box 190
SW7
071 584 3137

ISBN 85223 363 9

Phototypeset in Great Britain by
Tradespools Limited, Frome, Somerset
Printed and bound by New Interlitho s.p.a., Milan

Contents

Introduction

Gingerbread is said to be the oldest cake-bread in the world. Ginger was known in England before the Norman Conquest, and may have been brought over by the Romans via the trade-routes from the Orient and Africa.

Gingerbread biscuits were sold by pedlars at English country fairs and in street markets. At Bartholomew Fair they were called 'fairings' and sold at 20 a penny. The gingerbreads were popular as much for their delightful shapes as for the effect of their hot spices, which 'warmed the blood'. The biscuits were fashioned into animals and human shapes for both religious and secular occasions.

In the fifteenth century engraved rolling pins were used to form the gingerbread and these were later replaced by intricately carved wooden moulds. The expression, 'the gilt on the gingerbread', comes from the custom of gilding figures of kings and queens with Dutch leaf, as both ginger and gilt were popular in Elizabethan times.

Today gingerbread still holds its appeal, be it the fairytale Hansel and Gretel houses children dream of, or the little men with raisin eyes and buttons that are still found in every baker's shop. The gingerbreads in this book are really a modern extension of a most ancient form of creative bakery.

Acknowledgements
Many thanks to Wallace Heim, Roz Warner and Isabelle Lousada for their design and recipe suggestions, and to my mother, Patricia Lousada, for her generous help and advice with the cakes. Special thanks also to Xavier Loutreuil for his patient and constructive criticism through-out the making of this book.

All of the gingerbread biscuits in this book have been made from the same basic recipe. Instructions for cutting out shapes, baking and icing are given below in detail, and are not repeated elsewhere in the book. The photographs illustrate some of the possibilities and hopefully will serve to encourage many other imaginative uses.

Basic gingerbread recipe
175 g (6 oz) self-raising flour
100 g (4 oz) plain flour
1½ tbsp ground ginger
1½ tsp ground cinnamon
¼ tsp ground cloves
100 g (4 oz) caster sugar
75 g (3 oz) butter
1 egg

Sift the flour and spices in a large bowl and then stir in the caster sugar. Cut the butter into small pieces and rub into the dry ingredients with your fingers. Mix the egg, golden syrup and treacle together, pour into the flour mixture and mix to a smooth dough. Wrap in greaseproof paper and chill for at least 30 minutes in the refrigerator before using. This dough may also be frozen for future use.

Making paper patterns
Store-bought biscuit cutters come in many shapes and sizes and are quick to use, but it is easy and more fun to invent your own shapes for baking. For all the biscuits in this book I have first cut out a greaseproof paper pattern. This may be a solid shape, or may have a design cut out of it. Greaseproof paper is very good for two reasons: it does

not stick to the dough, and it can be used as tracing paper for transferring a drawn design onto the gingerbread.

Cutting out the gingerbread
Take a flat baking tray and cover it with a sheet of tin foil. If you do not have a flat baking sheet (with only one raised side) onto which you can roll the dough directly, roll the gingerbread out on to foil on a flat board, and after cutting, gently transfer the foil on to your baking sheet. Sprinkle a little flour on the foil, and roll the gingerbread out on it with a floured rolling pin. For small biscuits the dough can be used under 0.6 cm ($\frac{1}{4}$ in) thick, but for larger pieces, or for biscuits that are to be hung up roll the dough out at least 0.6 cm ($\frac{1}{4}$ in) thick, or the gingerbread will not be strong enough to support itself.

Place the paper pattern on to the dough and using a small sharp knife, cut around the edges, and then cut any inner patterns you may have. Gently peel off the paper. Remove excess dough around the biscuit, smoothing any edges which look frayed with your fingers as the gingerbread will not swell much in baking. Small holes may be punched in the dough with a piece of macaroni, pen lid or other hollow shape. At this point you may wish to decorate the biscuits with raisins or glacé cherries, or to try the appliqué method (see King and Queen).

Baking
Preheat oven to 180° C/350° F/mark 4. If the biscuits are small and are not going to hang or stand up, bake until golden, usually 12 to 15 minutes. If they are to be hung with ribbons or need to be more rigid, bake until the edges begin to darken slightly as the gingerbread will then be drier and less likely to bend or pick up moisture from the atmosphere.

When cool, peel foil off the back very carefully.

Icing
Royal icing has been used to decorate all the biscuits in this book. The egg white and icing sugar can be mixed to different thicknesses, depending on the finish that is required. The icing should be mixed up in small amounts, and the bowl kept covered with a damp cloth or cling film, as it dries out easily.

1 egg white
175–225 g (6–8 oz) icing sugar

Whisk the egg white in a medium-sized bowl with a fork. Gradually beat in the icing sugar, a tablespoon at a time, smoothing out any lumps against the side of the bowl.

If you wish to paint with the icing, beat until the mixture is the consistency of single cream, and still quite fluid. It can then be coloured and painted directly on to the biscuits with a small paint brush (see fans).

For the satin-finish icing, add more sugar and beat until the mixture is the consistency of double cream, is ribbony and not too stiff. A number 2 or 3 nozzle should be used. Outline the form and then fill in with icing. It will dry with a smooth solid finish (see small hearts).

For piping lines or writing, the icing must be quite stiff. Add more sugar until it forms peaks as it is beaten.

Making a paper piping bag

Little piping bags made of greaseproof paper into which the metal piping nozzles can be inserted are economical and quite easy to make. They offer the best control for delicate icing, and are very good if you want to use more than one colour at a time.

Take an oblong sheet of greaseproof paper 18 × 24 cm (7½ × 10 in). Fold as shown. Cut along fold. Hold the triangle at point C between thumb and forefinger. Form a cone by rolling D around to meet A. Wrap B around this cone until it meets A from the back. When the two cones are flush with one another fold the tops ADB down, and then fold them again. This will keep the bag secure. Snip off the end of the cone and drop in metal nozzle. It should protrude about 1.2 cm (½ in).

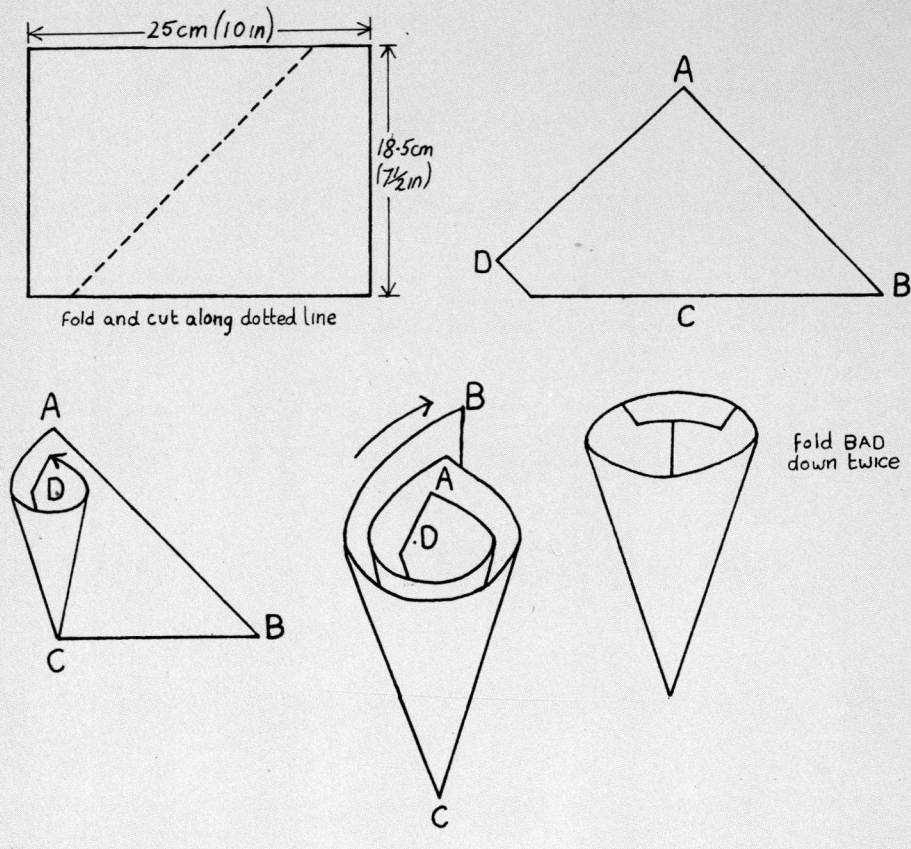

Filling a bag

Hold the bag securely as you spoon in the icing. Do not fill the bag more than half full. Close the top from the front, then fold in each side, and finally fold the top over. Hold the bag between the first two fingers and press out the icing with the thumb.

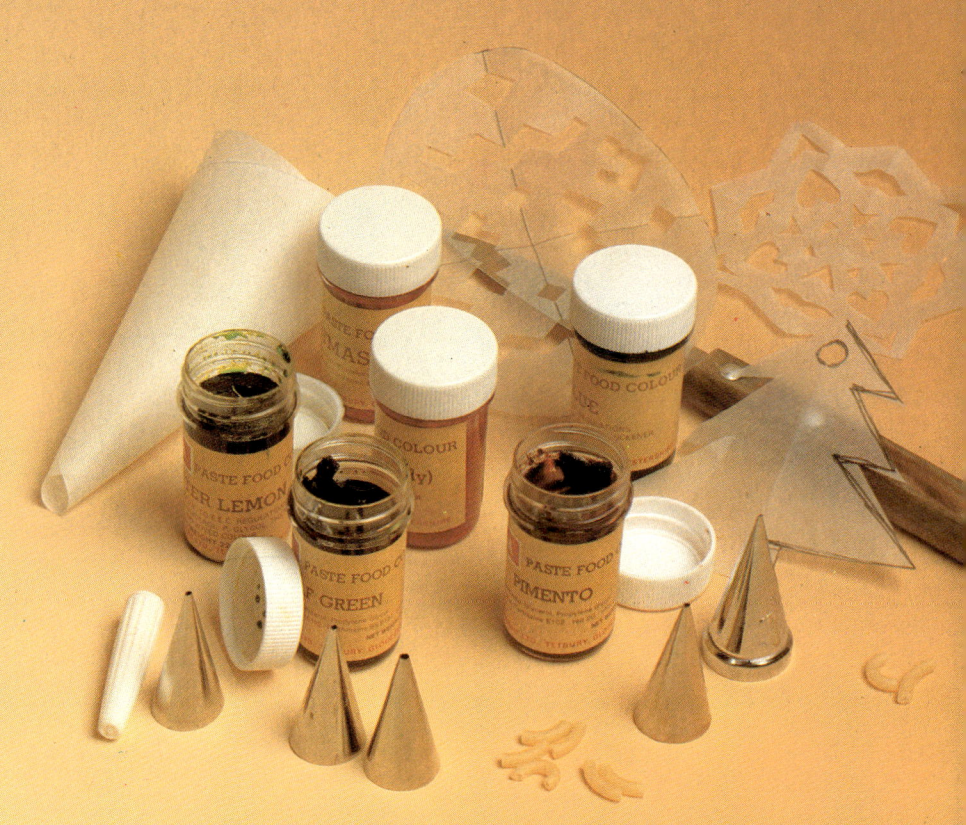

Colouring

A great range of colours is now available from good kitchen suppliers. Paste food colouring is preferable to liquid as it is very concentrated and does not thin the icing. In a small cup, mix a tiny amount of paste colour into a large tablespoonful of icing. Blend well and add more colour as needed. If you wish to work with several colours at a time it is a good idea to buy two or three each of nozzle numbers 1 and 2, as changing bags and nozzles for each new colour is time-consuming.

Sugar syrup

225 g (8 oz) sugar
150 ml ($\frac{1}{4}$ pint) water
a squeeze of lemon juice

Dissolve sugar in lemon juice and water over a low heat and then boil without stirring until a sugar thermometer reads 137° C/280° F. Be careful not to over-heat the mixture, or it will crack when cool.

Keeping gingerbread

Gingerbread dough freezes very well. It will keep in a refrigerator for two days. If you wish to preserve the biscuits after they have been baked and decorated, you may varnish them, but the coloured icing will fade after several weeks. The biscuits are obviously best eaten soon after baking, but gingerbread can be kept well in tins.

Measures

1 teaspoon (tsp) = 5 ml
1 tablespoon (tbsp) = 15 ml

Noah's Ark

This Noah's Ark is quite easy to make and children could have fun designing their own animal shapes to go with it. Roll out dough 0.6 cm ($\frac{1}{4}$ in) thick, cutting two of each animal from paper patterns. Bake for 12 to 15 minutes, and when cool, decorate in bright colours.

If designing the animals is a problem, particularly for children, draw the animals shown in the picture onto tracing paper or greaseproof paper, cut round the shapes and use these drawings as your templates or patterns. Enlarge or reduce the size using squared paper if necessary. Alternatively, children could find different types of animals in their favourite books.

When the figures are completed, arrange them two by two around the ark.

Leaves

A Thanksgiving dinner table can be most attractively decorated with autumnal gingerbread leaves. You can use real leaves as templates by tracing their shapes on greaseproof paper.

Roll out the dough 0.6 cm ($\frac{1}{4}$ in) thick, cut around templates, and bake biscuits for 12 to 15 minutes. Decorate with warm orange and brown icing, piping around contours or along the vein lines.

Wreath

This wreath has been assembled from two rounds of gingerbread, cut out of 0.6 cm ($\frac{1}{4}$ in) dough using paper patterns. The lower piece is larger, but has a smaller inner circle. The holes in the upper one have been punched out with a felt-tip pen lid before baking. Bake for 15 minutes, or until the edges begin to darken. If the gingerbread is undercooked it will not be sufficiently rigid to stand up.

After baking, carefully lace a length of soft ribbon through the holes, taking care to support the gingerbread with your hands so as not to break it as you pull the ribbon through. Ice both parts, and then stick them together with sugar syrup.

Fish

A box of these brightly-coloured fish would make a lovely present to take to a summer party or picnic at the seaside. The biscuits are cut from 0.6 cm ($\frac{1}{4}$ in) dough and baked for 12 to 15 minutes until golden brown, before being iced in suitably fishy colours.

The basic fish design can be traced from this picture onto greaseproof paper or tracing paper and enlarged if necessary using squared paper. For more difficult or unusual shapes, experiment by copying the different types of shells collected from beach expeditions or trace the more obscure types of fish from natural history illustrations. Early engravings in particular provide easy-to-copy designs.

For a party centrepiece, arrange the fish, shells and star fish on a greeny-blue background for the sea and shred clear cellophane into strips to make the waves.

Easter Egg Mobile

Decorating Easter eggs is fun for the whole family, and gingerbread eggs are no exception. Here a number of eggs of different styles have been assembled into a hanging mobile.

Roll out the dough 0.6 cm ($\frac{1}{4}$ in) thick and after cutting out the shapes punch a small hole near the top of each egg with a piece of macaroni. Bake until the biscuits harden and begin to darken slightly at the edges. This will ensure that the gingerbread does not bend when hung up. After icing, carefully attach a thread to the top of each egg.

To make the mobile, first balance the eggs visually by laying them out in position

on a table, with enough space for each one to hang freely. Tie them onto thin wooden rods and then adjust the balance by sliding the thread along the rods until they hang straight. Start at the bottom, finding the point of balance of each rod before attaching it to the one above and hang the mobile where it can swing gently.

Place Names

Place names are fun to make for a tea-party or children's birthday party. The shapes and icing colours can be chosen to go with a decorated tea service, or to fit the mood of a particular occasion.

Roll out dough 0.6 cm ($\frac{1}{4}$ in) thick. Cut out shapes making a few more than you may need in case of accidents. Bake for 12 to 15 minutes. Ice when cool, piping names on first and then the decorative border. If you wish, a gingerbread centrepiece may be made to go with them.

Labels

These delicious labels could be used to accompany a box of biscuits, or to tie on to Christmas or birthday presents. They are a good way of using up left-over dough.

Roll out dough 0.6 cm ($\frac{1}{4}$ in) thick. Cut out shape, and punch hole for ribbon before baking. Bake 12–15 minutes, or until dough is firm and has stopped puffing. Ice when cool.

Ice when cool and put the address on the other side of the label as an amusing afterthought.

If you are using the labels on baskets as presents, it is a nice idea to fill the baskets first with coloured tissue paper, perhaps using several different shades in coordinating colours. Shred the paper thinly and stuff gently into the baskets. Homemade biscuits, perhaps also made of gingerbread, can then be put in the baskets with little danger of their breaking.

25

Valentines

Home-made valentines are always the nicest ones to give, and iced gingerbread hearts can carry personal messages that are delicious as well as lovely to look at. Cut the hearts from 0.6 cm ($\frac{1}{4}$ in) dough and bake for 12 to 15 minutes.

The small hearts in the photograph were quickly iced in tones of red using soft icing which dries to a smooth satin finish. The more elaborate white piping was done with a number 1 nozzle and stiffer icing.

King and Queen

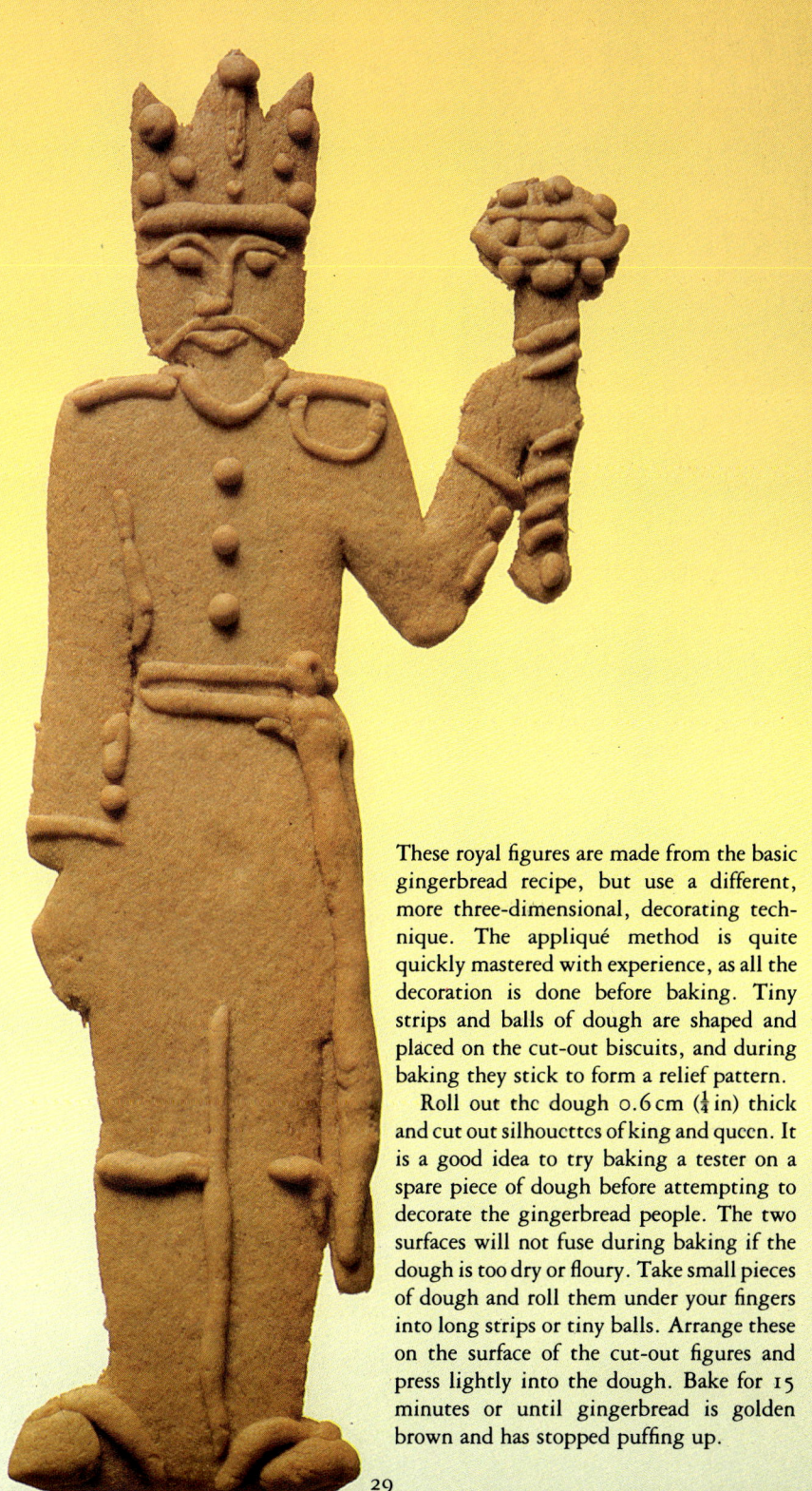

These royal figures are made from the basic gingerbread recipe, but use a different, more three-dimensional, decorating technique. The appliqué method is quite quickly mastered with experience, as all the decoration is done before baking. Tiny strips and balls of dough are shaped and placed on the cut-out biscuits, and during baking they stick to form a relief pattern.

Roll out the dough 0.6 cm ($\frac{1}{4}$ in) thick and cut out silhouettes of king and queen. It is a good idea to try baking a tester on a spare piece of dough before attempting to decorate the gingerbread people. The two surfaces will not fuse during baking if the dough is too dry or floury. Take small pieces of dough and roll them under your fingers into long strips or tiny balls. Arrange these on the surface of the cut-out figures and press lightly into the dough. Bake for 15 minutes or until gingerbread is golden brown and has stopped puffing up.

Christmas Decorations

These colourful Christmas decorations are easy to make and are particular favourites with children. Use them to brighten up your Christmas tree or wrap them in a pretty box for a delicious and economical present. Any number of simple shapes can be used, from the traditional American candy canes, to little presents decorated with children's names.

Roll the dough 0.6 cm (¼ in) thick, and after cutting out the shapes, punch a hole about 0.6 cm (¼ in) in diameter near the top of each biscuit with a small pen lid or sharp knife. Bake for 15 minutes, or until gingerbread begins to darken slightly. When cool, carefully thread a piece of ribbon through the hole and tie a small bow before icing the biscuits in festive colours.

For the snowflake templates take a round piece of paper, fold it over four times into a thin wedge, cut little shapes in from the edges and then open it out again.

Ginger and Apple Muffins

For about 18 × 5 cm (2 in) muffins

These spicy little cakes are kept moist by the apple and are delicious eaten hot or cold, and freshly buttered.

225 g (8 oz) plain flour
1½ tsp ground ginger
1¼ tsp cinnamon
¼ tsp ground cloves
¼ tsp baking soda
½ tsp salt
75 g (2½ oz) butter
100 g (3½ oz) sugar
1 egg
200 ml (6 fl oz) milk
125 ml (4 fl oz) molasses or treacle
40 g (1½ oz) butter
2 medium dessert apples, peeled, cored and sliced
(2 tbsp chopped stem ginger)

Preheat oven to 180°C/350°F/mark 4. Sift together the flour, spices, baking soda, baking powder and salt. In a large bowl cream butter and sugar. Mix in the egg and beat until light and fluffy. Combine the milk and molasses. Add the dry ingredients and the milk mixture alternately to the creamed butter. Stir after each addition only until blended.

Butter a large muffin tray. Drop a few small slices of apple into each muffin cup. You may also wish to sprinkle a little finely chopped stem ginger into each one. Spoon a large tablespoonful of the batter into each muffin cup, but do not fill them more than two-thirds full. Bake for 40 minutes or until a toothpick inserted in the centre comes out clean. Serve warm or cold, with butter if you wish.

American Hot Gingerbread

Serves 8

This most delicious cake is traditionally served warm, accompanied by whipped cream.

100 g (4 oz) butter
200 g (7 oz) sugar
2 eggs
1 tsp grated lemon or orange rind
200 g (7 oz) plain flour
1 tsp ground nutmeg
1 tsp baking soda
1½ tsp ground ginger
100 ml (3 fl oz) treacle
110 ml (4 fl oz) boiling water

Preheat oven to 180°C/350°F/mark 4. Grease and line a 22 cm (9 in) square baking tin with non-stick parchment paper. Cream the butter with the sugar until light and fluffy. Lightly beat the eggs with the fruit rind, and gradually mix into the butter. Sift the flour with the salt and spices. Mix the treacle with the boiling water. Add the sifted ingredients and the treacle alternately to the butter mixture.

Bake batter for 35–40 minutes. Allow to cool for 5 minutes before cutting into squares and serving warm, with whipped cream if you wish.

Gingernuts

For about 24 biscuits

100 g (4 oz) plain flour
a pinch of salt
1 tsp baking powder
1 tsp baking soda
1½ tsp ground ginger
½ tsp nutmeg
½ tsp cinnamon
50 g (2 oz) butter, cut into pieces
50 g (2 oz) caster sugar
2–3 tbsp golden syrup

Preheat oven to 180°C/350°F/mark 4. Sift flour, salt and spices together in a large bowl. Rub the butter into the dry ingredients. Stir in sugar. Warm the syrup until it is runny, and pour 2 tablespoons into the flour mixture. Mix with your hands to form a soft dough, adding the remaining golden syrup if necessary.

Roll walnut-sized pieces of the dough between your hands, and then in the caster sugar. Place them about 10 cm (4 in) apart on a well-greased baking tray. Flatten them slightly with a spatula before baking for 12–15 minutes. Remove biscuits with a spatula to a flat surface and allow to cool. Store in an airtight container.

For about 36 biscuits

125 ml (4 fl oz) golden syrup
100 g (3½ oz) caster sugar
100 g (3½ oz) butter, in small pieces
115 ml (3½ fl oz) double cream
50 g (2 oz) mixed peel, chopped
2 tsp ground ginger
1½ tsp ground cinnamon
1 tsp ground cardamon
225 g (8 oz) plain flour
1 tsp baking soda

Preheat the oven to 200°C/400°F/mark 6. Dissolve the sugar in the syrup over a low heat. Stir in the butter, then add the cream, peel and spices. Sift the flour with the baking soda and work in to the syrup mixture, adding just enough to make a firm dough.

Roll out the dough about 0.6 cm (¼ in) thick. Cut into small rounds and place on a well-greased baking tray. Bake for about 15 minutes until lightly browned

Ginger Roulade

Serves 8

This elegant dessert is easy to make. The sponge can be baked in advance, and the cream filling added a short time before serving.

100 g (3½ oz) plain flour
pinch of salt
4 eggs, separated
175 g (6 oz) sugar
2 tbsp treacle
2 tbsp boiling water
1½ tsp ground ginger
300 ml (½ pint) double cream
25 g (1 oz) stem ginger, chopped

Preheat oven to 200°C/400°F/mark 6. Grease and line a 30 × 40 cm (12 × 16 in) Swiss roll tin with non-stick parchment paper. Sift the flour with ground ginger and salt and set aside. Beat the egg yolks with two-thirds of the sugar until thick and light. Whisk the egg whites until stiff, add the remaining sugar, and whisk a few minutes longer until glossy. Using a metal spoon, fold the flour and egg whites into the yolk mixture by thirds. Dissolve treacle in boiling water, and fold into the mixture. Spread evenly in the prepared tin and bake for 8–10 minutes.

Loosen the edges with a knife before turning out onto a cloth covered with greaseproof paper which has been lightly sprinkled with icing sugar. Peel paper off back of the sponge, and roll the cake up inside cloth and paper. Leave until ready to use.

Before serving, whip the cream and add chopped ginger. Unroll sponge, and spread it evenly with the cream. Roll up again and refrigerate until served.

Pain d'Epice–French Gingerbread

To make one loaf

250 g (8 oz) rye flour
250 g (8 oz) plain flour
1 tsp salt
25 g (1 oz) fresh yeast or half quantity dried
300 ml ($\frac{1}{2}$ pint) lukewarm water
1 tsp brown sugar
250 ml (10 fl oz) honey
$1\frac{1}{2}$ tsp ground ginger
$1\frac{1}{2}$ tsp ground allspice

Place flour and salt together in a large bowl. Dissolve yeast in water and sugar. Pour yeast mixture into flour and, using a wooden spoon, stir from the centre, gradually drawing up all the flour. Knead for 5–6 minutes on a floured board. Return dough to bowl, cover with damp cloth, and leave in a warm place until doubled in volume, about $1\frac{1}{2}$ hours.

Punch the dough down and gradually knead in spices and honey. Prepare a loaf tin by lining it with 4 layers of paper and then a lining of non-stick greaseproof or parchment paper. Spoon the batter into the tin, and leave for about 45 minutes, or until dough rises to top of tin. Bake in a preheated oven 160°C/320°F/mark 3 for $2\frac{1}{2}$ hours, covering the top with foil during baking if top of loaf gets too brown. Cool in the tin before turning out. Keep the loaf tightly wrapped in cling film to retain moisture before serving.

Rich Ginger Cake

This traditional English ginger cake is rich
and sticky, and tastes best when eaten a few
days after baking.

100 g (4 oz) butter
100 g (4 oz) brown sugar
2 eggs
225 ml (8 fl oz) treacle
½ tsp bicarbonate of soda
200 g (8 oz) plain flour
1½ tsp ground ginger
½ tsp cinnamon
50 g (2 oz) chopped stem ginger
50 g (2 oz) sultanas
2 tbsp milk

Preheat oven to 180°C/350°F/mark 4.
Cream the butter and sugar together. Beat
in the eggs, one at a time, and then the
treacle. Sift the flour, spices and soda
together, add sultanas and chopped ginger,
and combine with treacle mixture. Beat in
the milk.

Butter and flour a 17 cm (7 in) cake tin,
and pour in the mixture. Bake for 1½ to 1¾
hours, depending on how moist you wish
the inside of the cake to be. Cool for 5
minutes in tin before turning out.

Ginger Pound Cake

250 g (9 oz) self-raising flour
2 tsp ground ginger
250 g (9 oz) butter
250 g (9 oz) sugar
4 eggs, separated
a pinch of salt
8 tbsp cognac
75 g (3 oz) stem ginger (in syrup) chopped

Preheat oven to 180°C/350°F/mark 4.
Grease and line a 22 cm (9 in) round deep
cake tin. Sift flour with ground ginger and
set aside. Cream butter with three-quarters
of sugar until light and fluffy. Add egg
yolks, one at a time, beating well after each
addition, then stir in the cognac. Whisk
egg whites with the salt until almost stiff,
then whisk in the remaining sugar and
continue whisking until whites are stiff and
glossy. Fold the egg whites and flour
alternately into the creamed mixture. Fold
in chopped stem ginger. Spoon mixture
into prepared tin and bake for about 50
minutes. Allow cake to cool in the tin for 30
minutes before turning out. When comple-
tely cool cake may be wrapped in foil and
stored in an airtight container.

Gingerbread House

To make this gingerbread house you will need a double quantity of the basic gingerbread recipe. First draw out the plans on squared or greaseproof paper, cutting out the windows and door. Roll out the gingerbread quite thickly at least 0.7 cm ($\frac{1}{3}$ in), and cut two of each of the three sections. Bake for 25–30 minutes, or until gingerbread has stopped puffing and is beginning to darken at edges. After baking for 15 minutes check that the windows are not closing up as they bake, and if necessary, straighten their edges with a small, sharp knife.

When cool, ice around the windows and door, and then add decorative tiles or brickwork as desired. Allow the royal icing time to set hard before assembling the house.

Assembling the house

Cut 8 strips of muslin or lawn 5 × 2.4 cm ($2\frac{1}{2}$ × 1 in). Boil the sugar syrup, and working quickly while it is still warm, paint along the side edges of the walls where they are to join one another. Holding the walls in place, dip strips of the fabric into the sugar syrup and use them to 'paper' over the cracks from the inside, two at each side. These will stop the walls from opening up and will make the house more stable. Paint more syrup along the top of the walls and stick the roof pieces to them. The gingerbread slabs will have warped slightly at the corners after baking but irregularities in the joins can be covered with royal icing after the house has been assembled.

A lovely effect can be obtained by placing a small night candle inside the house.

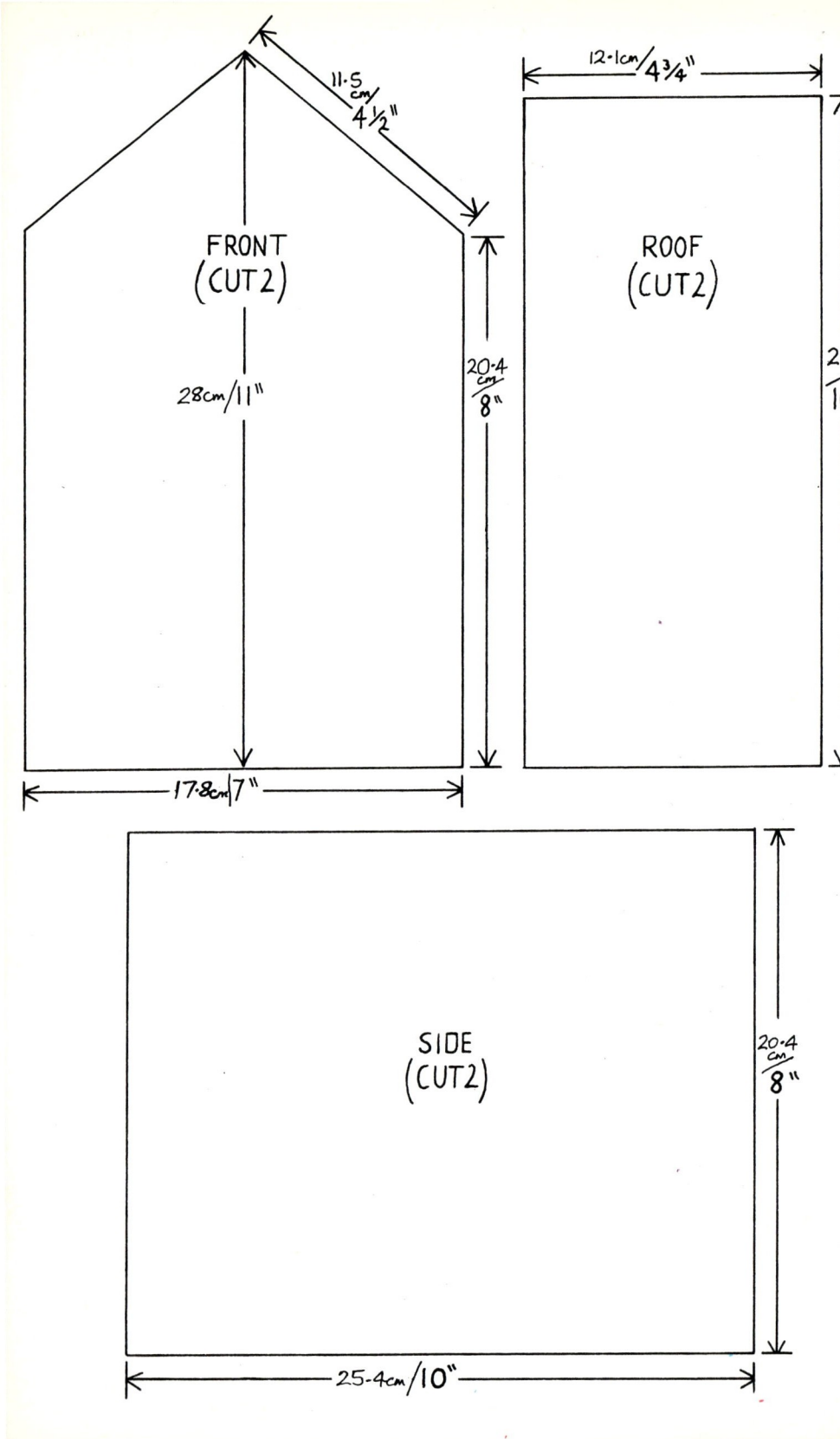

FRONT
(CUT 2)

11·5 cm / 4½"

28cm/11"

20·4 cm / 8"

17·8cm/7"

ROOF
(CUT 2)

12·1cm / 4¾"

26cm / 10.

SIDE
(CUT 2)

20·4 cm / 8"

25·4cm/10"

SI4 NT.